Table of contents

Introduction to Balancing Conflicting Interests

This booklet is aimed at AQA Unit 4C; however the theory of law, which is called *jurisprudence*, is a compulsory part of most law degrees. The various concepts of law are *synoptic*. This means they connect to other areas of study, not just the substantive law, but its institutions and procedures. In this booklet, we cover 'Balancing Conflicting Interests'. You will be expected to show your understanding of this by not only relating it to the substantive law and procedures, but also to contemporary issues. You will find plenty of examples in this booklet.

A few introductory examples

Legal procedures often involve an attempt to balance the interests of the individual with the public interest, especially in criminal law where society as a whole is affected by criminal behaviour.

The public interest in being safe from harm is seen in the mandatory life sentence for murder and other sentencing policies, especially deterrent sentences and also in the refusal of bail for murder cases. The public interest is also seen in the fact that consultations with the public often precede an Act of Parliament.

However, private interests are also taken into account by allowing defences to crimes in certain circumstances, by providing victims of violence with compensation, by putting the burden of proof on the prosecution, by improving access to justice, by offering financial assistance and trial by jury. In addition, the Bail Act, the Criminal Cases Review Commission and the appeals system generally offer protection to the individual.

Contemporary issues involving conflicting interests include the separation of Siamese twins, the right to die, gay marriage and the fight against terrorism.

More such examples, along with examples in criminal law, tort and contract are given later.

Many academics, philosophers and judges have written about the different concepts of law, and there is often disagreement between them.

Examination tip

You are not expected to 'take sides' when discussing legal or academic views and you may wish to state your own opinion. However, if you do, be sure to back this up with reference to relevant cases and to a theorist if possible. The main thing when it comes to the exam is to have a clear focus and keep your answer centred on the specific question asked, i.e., keep your answer and examples relevant and, where possible, refer to a theorist or two to support what you say.

I have used a range of case examples and hopefully you will be familiar with many of them. However, space is limited because I want to include plenty of examples and tasks, so I have not included the full facts. If a case is unfamiliar but you feel you would like to use it to illustrate a point you will need to look it up. Most should be in your text book, and all appear in the relevant chapters of my own books on Units 3A and 4C as well as in the other books in this '*the law explained*' series.

Essay pointer

You always need cases and examples to illustrate and support what you say in an essay. Where possible also refer to a theorist on the area to develop your points. You can also develop your point by arguing for and against the decision, which shows you are trying to provide a balanced view. Another idea is to learn and fully understand cases that can be used for several different concepts, because you can use the same one in different questions – as long as you change the focus.

Example

We can look at how the case of **Brown** can be used to discuss each of the five concepts in Unit 4C AQA Law. This is a very brief outline, as you may not have covered all these concepts. However, it should give you an idea of how you can use a case and then adapt and develop it to different situations – a bit like judges do with law.

Concept	Aspect of the case that relates to this concept	Mention of a theorist where possible
Law and Morals	Whether sexual violence in private should be regulated by law rather than purely a matter of morality	**Devlin** would say 'yes' because immoral acts undermine the fabric of society, even when done in private **Hart** would say 'no' because law and morals should be kept separate **Mill** might say 'yes' because he believed in non-interference in individual rights, but could say 'no' because he added 'unless doing so could harm others'
Law and Justice	Whether justice is achieved by imposing legal sanctions against certain behaviour even if it occurs in private	The above could be used again but also a **Utilitarian** would want to see the greatest benefit for the greatest number so could argue that this is achieved by banning the behaviour of the minority to protect society as a whole
Judicial Creativity	Earlier cases conflicted on whether consent was a defence to serious injuries, the majority indicated the ratio was that it was not	Where a *ratio* is unclear, later judges can select the most appropriate or can distinguish the case on the facts. **Professor Goodhard** said, *"It is by his choice of material facts that the judge creates law"* Arguably with such a serious crime Parliament rather than unelected judges should create the law
Fault	It was unclear whether the decision was based on the amount of harm or whether the harm was intentional	*Mens rea* is an important element of criminal law and where harm is committed with intent it should be penalised The acts had been consented to, so it is wrong that the law penalised the behaviour. Even though there was MR the consent defence should have succeeded
Balancing Conflicting Interests	The interests of the public to be protected from violence had to be balanced against the interests of the individuals to act as they pleased in private	**Devlin** would say that society had to be protected from evil, as did some of the judges in **Brown**. **Lord Lowry** said sadomasochism was *"not conducive to the welfare of society"*, and so a **Utilitarian** might agree with the decision. **Pound** believed that public and private interests should not be balanced against each other as the public interest will always prevail, as seen here

The tasks are intended to reinforce your learning so do these as you go along. The answers are at the end of the booklet. Refer to these for revision and examination practice. I have included a few quotes where appropriate, so use these too; they show that you know what judges have to say about the law.

Balancing Conflicting Interests

"There is a contest here between the interest of the public at large and the interest of a private individual" – Lord Denning MR in **Miller v Jackson 1977**

What is an interest?

An interest is similar to a right. With most rights come corresponding duties. Thus in criminal and tort law we have a right not to be harmed and a duty not to harm others. This imposes a corresponding duty on others not to cause harm, whether in criminal law or through negligence. In the tort of nuisance there is a right to quiet enjoyment of your land and a duty not to interfere with other people's rights to such enjoyment. In contract law there is a right to receive goods and a duty to pay the agreed price. The other party to the contract has a corresponding duty to supply the goods and a right to receive payment.

So the law protects people's rights by imposing a duty on others not to interfere with those rights. When those rights or interests come into conflict the law must balance them in an attempt to achieve justice. Also taken into the balance are the interests of society as a whole: the public interest.

Essay pointer

As balancing interests can be a way to achieve justice, the theories of justice can be referred to in an essay. This will give more depth to an essay than merely analysing the interests themselves (see Task 2 for an example). It is also a good way to evaluate whether the law has been effective in balancing interests, e.g., you can discuss whether the law has achieved distributive justice or justice according to a Utilitarian in a particular case or process.

Examination tip

You will need to identify and illustrate how competing interests are weighed up and balanced during the making and application of the law. There will be plenty of examples found in this booklet but when looking at a new case or procedure try to work out what the competing interests are and how the law has balanced them.

Task 1

Following on from the above examination tip make a few notes on any recent case or procedure you have come across and note down not only what the interests were and how the law balanced them but also whether this was an appropriate balance and achieved justice.

Public and private interests

Private interests are individual interests and these can conflict in many areas of life, e.g., when deciding which TV programmes to watch or when suing a manufacture for producing faulty goods. When the conflict involves a legal issue the law must resolve the conflict. It does this by balancing the individual interests against each other, and also against those of society (the public interest). Where there is a conflict between private and public interests, private interests may be subordinated to the public interest, i.e., those of the community. The utilitarian theory of maximising happiness can be seen in many legal decisions involving the public interest.

Example

If more people are made happy by a decision then a Utilitarian would see any conflicting interests as being fairly balanced. However it is total happiness not the number of people that matters so if one person is very unhappy and several others only mildly unhappy then the balance should be in favour of that one person. This is not seen very often in practice because community, or public, interests usually dominate. Thus in **Miller v Jackson** a woman whose life was made miserable by cricket balls being hit into her garden was refused an injunction to stop it. The community interest prevailed. The opening quote came from this case and shows that the private interests (Mrs Miller's) were balanced not only against another private interest (that of the cricket club) but also against the public interest (society as a whole benefits from such activities). There are many cases where the public interest prevails because society as a whole gains a benefit from an activity at the expense of the discomfort of a few individuals. Examples include building airports, motorways, recycling facilities, sewage treatment plants – in fact most such activities that provide a public benefit will cause discomfort to those nearby, as seen in the tort of nuisance.

As a Utilitarian, Bentham saw the law as attempting to achieve maximum happiness, or 'the greatest good'. His theories of justice influenced the work of **Jhering**, another Utilitarian. Jhering produced a theory to explain how the law should balance interests, with an emphasis on the needs of society. Theories of justice attempt to *define* justice. Theories on balancing conflicting interests attempt to explain what interests are and how the law can/should balance them to *achieve* justice. For more on the theories of justice see 'Law and Justice the law explained' or 'Unit 4C Concepts of Law'.

Examination tip

Try to relate the idea of balancing conflicting interests to a theory of justice when illustrating an examination answer. A *Utilitarian*, like Bentham, might say justice is best achieved by balancing the interests to ensure the greatest good for the greatest number. A *Marxist* would want to ensure that any balancing act resulted in individuals receiving what they need whilst contributing what they can. Aristotle would suggest that the law should balance competing interests by redistributing benefits and burdens fairly across society. As an *Egalitarian,* Rawls would want any redistribution to be equal. Nozick would claim that any state-initiated redistribution was unjust.

Task 2

Remind yourself of Aristotle's theory of distributive justice. How could you use this theory to support the decision of the court in **Miller v Jackson** not to award an injunction?

Jhering emphasised the needs of society when balancing interests. He saw law as a form of social engineering, ordering the way society behaved. Whether the law was just was measured by how far it achieved a proper balance in resolving the conflict in society between people's social interests and people's individual interests. Jhering's work was in turn relied on by one of the main writers on the subject of conflicting interests, the American academic lawyer, Roscoe Pound.

Roscoe Pound

Pound regarded law as an engineering tool, a form of social control. He studied law's position in society and how it could be used to 'engineer' a balance between the different interests within society. He developed the theory of 'social engineering'. Where interests are in conflict, the law will try to engineer a balance which will achieve social cohesion. The purpose of law is to satisfy as many interests as possible. The maximum number of wants satisfied with the minimum amount of friction and waste. Where interests conflicted, they had to be weighed, or balanced, against each other with the aim of satisfying as many as possible. Pound developed Jhering's theory of using the law to achieve a balance, but argued that interests could only be balanced on the same level. Thus, social interests (public interests) should not be balanced against individual interests (private interests), only other social interests, and *vice versa*.

Example

An example would be the debate on smoking in public. In Pound's view, the individual interests of those who favour a ban (avoiding passive smoking) can be balanced against the interests of those who don't think the law should interfere (freedom of choice), as they are on the same level, but not against the wider social interests. Alternatively, the social benefits (lots of tax on cigarettes which helps pay for other social benefits) and burdens (health problems, burden on the health service) can be balanced against each other, but these shouldn't be balanced against the individual's interests.

Neither Parliament nor the courts has always followed Pound's theory in so far as balancing interests only on the same level is concerned.

Example

During the debates which preceded the smoking ban, both social and individual interests were taken into account. This would conflict with Pound's view of not balancing public against private interests but is a clear example of how the law has been used to 'engineer' the way society behaves – to stop people smoking.

Examination tip

A common point made in examiners' reports is that candidates often fail to refer to the wider impact on society when the law balances conflicting interests. There are plenty of examples of cases and procedures where the public interest is taken into account so try to discuss interests outside the obvious claimant/defendant or defendant/victim roles. These are certainly valid examples but there are wider issues which need to be discussed for higher-range marks.

Examples

The public interest is often taken into account when making and applying criminal law. This is seen particularly clearly in relation to defences, e.g., it is not seen as in the public interest to allow voluntary intoxication as a defence. In **O'Grady** the public interest in being protected from violence outweighed his private interest in not being liable for a crime where he did not know what he was doing, so arguably lacked *mens rea*. Nor is it in the public interest to allow consent as a defence to causing serious harm (**Brown**) or death (**Pretty**). Again, in these cases the public interest dominates.

The idea of the law acting to resolve conflict, and 'engineering' a balance between competing interests, is seen in many areas.

The engineering tools

The 'engineering tools' the law uses to try to balance the interests are:

the substantive law

the legal process

sanctions and remedies

As you look at the examples in each of these, don't forget to consider what interests are in conflict, how they are being balanced and whether a just balance is achieved.

The substantive law

Whichever area of law you are studying, you'll find plenty of cases to choose from. Here are a few ideas.

Crime

The public interest is taken into account when making and applying criminal law; this is seen particularly clearly in relation to defences, e.g., that it is not in the public interest to allow voluntary intoxication as a defence (**O'Grady**) or to allow consent as a defence to causing serious harm

(**Brown**) or death (**Pretty**). In these cases the public interest in being protected from violence dominates.

Here are a few examples, there are plenty more so use ones that you feel most comfortable explaining.

Bratty v A-G for Northern Ireland 1963	• Lord Denning said a disorder which led to violence and was prone to recur was "the sort of disease for which a person should be retained in hospital rather than be given an unqualified acquittal." The law on insanity can be used to protect society.
O' Grady 1987	• "There are two competing interests. On the one hand the interest of D who has only acted according to what he believed to be necessary to protect himself, and on the other hand that of the public in general, and the victim in particular who, probably through no fault of his own, has been injured or perhaps killed because of D's drunken mistake." CA
R v R 1991	• Society had moved on, so the rule of precedent to treat like cases alike was subordinated to the interests of society, and the victim, to be protected.
Brown 1994	• The Lords' decision was partly based on the need to protect society from what was seen as deviant behaviour. This outweighed the rights of the individuals to do what they liked with their own bodies. Lord Templeman said society was entitled to protect itself against a cult of violence.
Wilson 1996	• Society did not need protecting so the balance tipped in favour of D.
Cook 2008 / Freaney 2011	• The defence of diminished responsibility allows a balance to be struck between punishing killing and recognising the interests of D, as well as the victim and her family who had supported his actions.

Contract

Contract law is based on the idea of agreement. In general the courts are reluctant to interfere in order to engineer a balance of interests, preferring to allow the parties freedom to contract as they wish. However, there are times when a person's interests may need protecting, particularly where one party is in a weaker position than the other. Again, what follows are just a few examples, and it is best to use ones that you feel comfortable explaining.

The Moorcock 1889	• The court may impose terms into a contract to engineer a just balance and ensure 'business efficacy'.
Oscar Chess Ltd v Willams1957	• A statement by a seller as to a car's age was held to be a representation, not a term. Compare this to **Dick Bentley Productions v Harold Smith Motors Ltd 1965**, where a statement that a car had only done 20,000 miles was held to be a term. The non-expert needs greater protection than the specialist.
Unfair Contract Terms Act 1977	• This and other consumer protection law attempts to achieve a just balance by giving protection to a consumer when dealing with a business, which is in a more powerful position.
Williams v Roffey 1990	• The court was prepared to weigh up the various interests in finding consideration. The act of finishing the work was enough to enforce the offer of extra payment, even though this was no more than had been agreed. It was a just balance based on the reality of the situation.
Wessanen Foods Ltd v Jofson Ltd 2006	• The court felt that in relation to a business agreement where the parties had equality of bargaining power an exclusion clause was reasonable. This achieves a balance between protection and non-interference. The courts are less likely to interfere in a contract where the parties deal on equal terms.

Tort

Tort provides plenty of examples. In proving a **duty of care** in negligence the courts will ask whether it is fair, just and reasonable to impose a duty on policy grounds. This involves balancing the right of C to compensation not only against the cost to D, but also against the wider community interests. This is particularly evident in cases involving the police, rescue services, hospitals and schools where compensation would usually come from public funds (i.e., tax-payers). Various factors are balanced against each other when proving **breach of duty**, including any benefit to society, and the **Compensation Act 2006** attempts to protect people from being sued when they are undertaking a 'desirable activity', such as school trips and sports. The **Consumer Protection Act 1987** was put in place in order to protect the interests of consumers, specifically those who have suffered some sort of harm due to a faulty product. The Act addresses the imbalance between the parties in such situations, where a consumer is in a weaker position in comparison to a manufacturer with greater resources.

A particularly good area to explore conflicting interests is the tort of **nuisance**. In **Hunter v Canary Wharf 1997**, nuisance was said to involve *"striking a balance between the interests of neighbours"*, so all nuisance cases involve an attempt to balance competing interests. One person's freedom can be another's misery.

Examples

I work late in a nightclub and when I get back to my flat I want to relax and enjoy some music. My right to play music at 3 a.m. has to be balanced against the rights of others in the apartment block to a good night's sleep.

Mrs Jones likes her privacy so has grown large trees all round her garden. Her neighbour Mrs Smith likes gardening but her plants won't grow because they get no sun. Both women have a right to enjoyment of their land and these rights, or interests, are in conflict.

If any of the people affected by the actions of their neighbours took the situation to court, the court would have to balance the competing rights to attempt to come to a fair solution.

Here are some case examples.

Christie v Davey 1893	• balancing the right of one neighbour to give piano lessons against the other's right to quiet enjoyment of their property
Latimer v AEC 1952	• the right of an individual to compensation is subordinated to the wider community interest of keeping the factory open
Watts v Herts CC 1954	• balancing the right of an individual to compensation against the fact that it was a rescue operation. As it was the Fire Service any compensation would come from public funds
Miller v Jackson 1977	• private interests (C's right to quiet enjoyment) were again subordinated to community interests (the playing of cricket)
Hill v Chief Constable of West Yorkshire 1988	• balancing the right of an individual to compensation against the wider community interests in deciding it was not 'fair' to impose a duty on police
Harris v Perry 2008	• a balance has to be struck between the interests of children being able to play, and the interests of the community as a whole in being protected from harm

Task 3

Choose a case on your area of study, or use one of my examples. Write a note of the facts and the judgement. Then add a paragraph on how, and whether, you think that the court achieved an appropriate balance between the competing interests.

Essay pointer

It can be argued that if a decision is made on the basis of doing right in the particular circumstances, rather than always doing the same regardless of the circumstances, then consistency may be lost. Consider whether the law is achieving justice at the expense of certainty when balancing competing interests. Bringing in a theory of justice to an essay shows you have looked at the big picture. An example would be that Mill's view of justice was that the law should only restrict a person's freedoms where harm could be caused to others. Thus when balancing conflicting interest this should be taken into account and the private interest of the person acting should be given more weight if no-one else would be harmed by that action.

The legal process

Conflicting interests will be seen at various stages during the law-making process. The government has to balance these when formulating policy, as with the consultations preceding the **Human Fertilisation and Embryology Act 2008** which followed the **Quintavalle** case.

At the next stage, the **Human Rights Act 1998** affects the balance between the potentially conflicting interests of the state and the people. This **Act** ensures that rights under the **European Convention on Human Rights (ECHR)** are taken into account when the policy is drafted into a Bill. Also, the Green and White consultation papers allow for different interest groups to be consulted at this stage too. The resulting law may well reflect their interests. During the process of the Bill becoming an Act, various bodies will be lobbying Members of Parliament to vote in their interests. Finally, judges have to interpret and apply an Act once it becomes law. The **Human Rights Act** has an influence on the balance here too because judges must take the **ECHR** into account when interpreting laws.

The right to a trial by jury has to be balanced against the cost of providing such trials. In the interests of justice the balance has usually tipped in favour of the individual's right to a fair trial (the private interest). A bill to remove complex fraud trials from this was enacted but never became law. The **Protection of Freedoms Act 2012** repeals the provisions which allowed for complex fraud trials to be heard without a jury. However, it does not affect the **Criminal Justice Act 2003**, which allows for trial without jury where there are fears of jury tampering. Here the balance has moved away from the private interest and the first trial without jury in a major criminal case took place in January 2010. Several procedures are put in place in an attempt to provide a fair balance between public and private interests, e.g., the police have powers to stop and search people to assist in their fight against crime, but the **Police and Criminal Evidence Act** limits those powers to protect the individual.

Here are a few more examples.

Alternative Dispute Resolution	• An attempt to balance interests through negotiation, mediation and conciliation. The Woolf reforms also ensure judges act as mediators.
Trials	• The right of D to be tried by ordinary people balanced against the cost to society of a jury trial.
Bail	• There is a presumption that bail should be granted in most cases. This achieves greater justice for the accused, who is deemed innocent until found guilty. The presumption does not apply in murder and rape cases. D's rights are subordinated to those of society to be protected from such serious crimes.
Precedent	• The need for certainty is balanced against the need to do justice in a particular case. Thus the strict rule of 'stare decisis' is tempered by the rules on overruling and distinguishing. In **Gemmell and Richard 2003** the HL used the **1966 Practice Statement** to overrule itself. The principle of treating like cases alike is sacrificed in the interest of justice.

Sanctions and remedies

These will be relevant when considering *how* a balance is achieved. The public interest is often seen in sentencing (sanctions) policy. When deciding on appropriate remedies the judge will try to engineer what Pound called '*the maximum number of wants with the minimum amount of friction and waste*'.

Sentencing

It has been argued that whole-life sentences, given for 'exceptionally serious offences', where there is no possibility of review or release are against the **European Convention on Human Rights**. However, in **McLoughlin and Newell 2014**, the CA held that, as the **Crime (Sentences) Act 1997** allows for release in exceptional circumstances on compassionate grounds (e.g., where a prisoner is terminally ill), whole life sentences are within the law. Seriously violent offenders endanger society as a whole, so the public interest in being safe from such offenders outweighs their private interest in being locked up without hope of release.

A deterrent sentence may sacrifice the interests of the particular D to those of society. For example, a custodial sentence may be given where the offence does not really warrant one. It is used to stop re-offending and deter others from offending, thus protecting society. A crime against children or the elderly often leads to a public demand for a harsher sentence; here the community interest may outweigh D's. V's interests are also weighed in the balance, and courts will take into account a Victim Impact Statement, showing the effect of the crime on V.

Remedies

When deciding on appropriate remedies, especially equitable ones, the judge must balance the competing rights of the individual parties in an attempt to find a just solution. The community interest may affect the balance. The law acts as mediator, and the judge will attempt to achieve a compromise which will most satisfy all interests.

Example

In **Miller v Jackson**, the court allowed her claim but refused to grant an injunction to stop the cricket. She received damages to compensate her for past and future inconvenience but an injunction was refused, which meant the cricket could continue.

Task 4

Choose 3 procedures. Write down the competing interests involved and how the law engineered a balance between these interests. Now consider which theories of justice would most support this balance. Keep this for revision of both areas.

Current affairs

The law is involved in many more areas than you might realise, and the papers carry stories every day that can be used to illustrate an essay. It is unlikely that people will agree on issues like fox hunting, smoking and whether a school can tell the children what to eat or what not to watch on TV, so there will always be a lot of debate when the law gets involved in such areas.

Examination tip

Examiners like to see reference to contemporary examples. As well as using well-known cases from your text-book, keep an eye out for other instances of conflicting interests in the media which you could use to illustrate an essay.

Here are a few examples which show that the concept of balancing conflicting interests is still important in the 21st century.

'Designer' babies

Several interests were in conflict in **Quintavalle v Human Fertilisation and Embryology Authority 2005**. The pressure group (CORE) argued that tissue typing was unethical but the director of the clinic where the treatment took place said *"ethical concerns over creating children with specific genetic material were outweighed by the benefits"*. The HL had to try to find a balance between the interests of the parents, the child who was ill, the unborn child, those who argued the treatment infringed the right to life and those who were 'pro-choice'. Whilst recognising the case raised *"profound ethical questions"*, the HL held that the Act allowed tissue typing, but in limited circumstances.

There is a clear overlap with morals so other issues such as euthanasia, assisted suicide and anorexia can be discussed. However, you will need to change the emphasis to one involving the competing interests rather than the issue of morals, so concentrate on considering whose interests the law was trying to protect and whether it was successful in doing so. Controversial cases like this are useful in illustrating not only how the courts are required to balance competing interests, but also in demonstrating the difficulties in doing so.

Example

In assisted suicide cases, there are privates interests in conflict and there is also a conflict between the private and public interests. The private interests are the individuals' right to choose the time and manner of their own death against the right to be protected from others who may have a reason to encourage that death. A loved one may want to help when asked (**Purdy**, **Niklinson**), but it is possible others may have less compassionate motives and could encourage someone to die because they have become a burden, or because they will gain from that person's death. The public interest lies in the argument that taking a life for any reason diminishes society as a whole, and also in the point above that people in general may need protection. Law is a tool for engineering a fair balance between competing interests but these examples show the difficulties in doing so, one of the reasons no government has been prepared to produce a law allowing euthanasia in any form. Until Parliament acts, judges will have to try to balance these interests to protect the majority and base legal decisions on what is best for society as a whole. The individual in the case may feel that justice has not been achieved in this balancing act but, as a Utilitarian would argue, the law should aim to achieve the greatest overall benefit.

Where opinion on a subject is so divided it is almost impossible to satisfy the interests of any particular group, and neither Parliament nor the courts can be said to be wholly successful in resolving the conflicts. On the other hand, although the law is sometimes an imperfect tool, it is arguably the best one for balancing interests against each other, as it is more likely to be impartial when reaching any decision.

There are many conflicting freedoms under the **ECHR**. These are now part of UK law and have to be balanced against each other.

Privacy v freedom of expression

There have been many cases arguing the conflicting interests of freedom to a private life for public figures, and freedom of expression for those who wish to write about those lives. In **Campbell v MGN 2004**, the HL held that her right to privacy under **Article 8 ECHR** outweighed MGN's right to freedom of expression under **Article 10**. A case where the balance tipped the other way involved the footballer Rio Ferdinand. In **Ferdinand v MGN Ltd 2011**, he tried to prevent publication of an article alleging that he had had an affair. In several articles and in his autobiography he had given the impression that he was a family man and had given up 'playing around'. He was also the England captain, so his conduct was of special interest to the public. The court held that the balance of interest lay in protecting the publisher's freedom of expression over the footballer's right to privacy. Similar conflicts of interest arose in **Murray v Express Newspapers** where JK Rowling won a case brought on behalf of her young son against a photographic agency for publishing secretly taken photographs of him.

In another case involving photographs of a child, **AAA v Associated Newspapers 2013**, weight was again given to the interests of the child, who had an expectation of privacy, but the court held that this was not absolute. Some information had already been published so it was a reduced expectation of privacy that had to be balanced against the public interest in being informed (a high profile politician was allegedly the father of the child) and the freedom of expression of the publisher. In this case the judge had decided the balance lay in favour of the public and the publisher and refused an injunction. The CA upheld the decision and said that where a judge had carefully balanced the competing interests of the parties (again **Articles 8** and **10** of the **ECHR**) an appeal court should not normally interfere unless it was clearly wrong or unreasonable. These cases, along with the appeals and reversals in **Douglas v Hello!,** in respect of Michael Douglas and Catherine Zeta-Jones' wedding photographs, highlight the difficulties of getting the balance right.

Terrorism

The **Anti-terrorism, Crime and Security Act 2001** allowed the Home Secretary to detain indefinitely foreign nationals suspected of terrorism, without charge or trial.

The then Prime Minister, Tony Blair, said he had to

> *"... weigh the wrong which is being done to a tradition in history of the primacy of law versus the wrong that would be done were any of these terrorist organisations to succeed in their ambitions."*

The Law Society said

> *"We recognise the government has a difficult balancing act. But it is essential that emergency terror legislation protects the country without compromising the government's duty to uphold fairness and justice."*

The **Act** was passed and in an appeal in 2004 by several suspects who had been held for three years without trial, the HL held it was against the rule of law and breached the **ECHR**.

Lord Hoffman said, in response to government arguments that the act was necessary to protect the life of the nation,

> *"The real threat to the life of the nation ... comes not from terrorism but from laws such as these".*

He indicated that terrorism had succeeded if it meant the country rejected the rule of law in response to threats of terrorism.

The right balance has been hard to achieve. The **Terrorism Act 2006** removed the indefinite detention but allowed for suspects to be held without charge for 28 days. This was increased to 42 days by the **Counter-Terrorism Act 2008**. The **Protection of Freedoms Act 2012** has reduced it to 14 days. The interests of society to be protected have to be balanced not only against the suspect's rights, but also against the other interests of society in living in a free and fair state, and of justice as a whole. We all want to be safe, but most people do not want to live in a society that can lock people up without any charges being brought against them. A criminal trial is the proper place to decide these issues.

Most of the freedoms (another word for interests or rights) under the **ECHR** have what are called 'derogations'. This means that they may be sacrificed in the interests of, e.g., state security or public health. In this case individual rights are subordinated to the interests of the state. Freedom of expression not only has to be balanced against an individual's right to a private life as we saw above, but also against the public interest, so there are laws which restrict this freedom, e.g., the **Official Secrets Act**, blasphemy and censorship laws, defamation laws etc. We also saw above that freedom of movement can be restricted by anti-terrorism laws in the interests of security. In all criminal cases there is a restriction on this freedom as a suspect can be detained for certain amounts of time without charge, even though supposedly innocent until found guilty in a court of law.

It is not always clear what an appropriate balance *is*. Look at the notes you made for tasks 1 and 3. Did the laws you chose achieve an appropriate balance? Was justice achieved? For everyone or just one of the people involved? These are difficult issues and it is unlikely the law will always get it right. It is often the case in life that if you try to please everybody you end up pleasing nobody and the law is no different. Keep your notes for use in an essay where you may need to discuss the difficulties the law faces in balancing interests effectively.

Task 5

Would it be acceptable to torture a suspected bomber to get the location of a bomb which could kill hundreds of people? Apply the utilitarian theory of justice. Now go on to consider whether it is in the interests of society and whether this outweighs those of the individual? Is society itself degraded by such treatment? Should people even be locked up without being charged?

Don't panic, there is no 'right answer' here. Just jot down your thoughts.

Essay pointer

It is a good idea when discussing any of the concepts of law to try to take a balanced view. One way to show you have done this is to produce an argument for and against a particular point. Complete the next task for an example.

Task 6

You produced an argument in support of the decision in **Miller** for Task 2. Now use the same theory of distributive justice to argue that the decision did not achieve a fair balance and comment on how Pound's theory could have provided a more appropriate balance.

Summary

How and when can interests conflict?

How does this conflict of interests relate to other areas such as legal processes and substantive law?

Pound's theory of balancing conflicting interests:

Law is an engineering tool

It can be used to engineer how society behaves

Public and private interests should not be balanced against each other

Has the law achieved a fair balance?

Has justice been achieved?

In whose view has justice been achieved (e.g., utilitarianism, distributive justice, natural law)?

Self-test questions

What does Pound mean by saying that law is an engineering tool?

*Give one example from tort, contract **or** crime **and** one from the legal process where you can explain the competing interests*

*What effect does the **Human Rights Act** have on court cases?*

How would a Utilitarian engineer the balance between conflicting interests?

*What happened in **Miller v Jackson** and whose interests prevailed?*

Revision

A general guide to revision

The first and foremost rule for revision is to start early. Too many students leave it until the last minute and then get in a panic. If you take it gently and organise your time properly you will feel a lot more calm and confident when exam time comes. Make a plan of what you want to cover each day and try to stick to it. Don't forget to include some breaks in your schedule, if you are tired it will be harder to retain the material you have been revising.

Here are a few tips for revision techniques

Go through your notes and try to summarise them

For the substantive law, learn the key cases, as these are essential

Make sure you understand how the judge has applied the law to the facts so you can do the same in an examination scenario (although not needed for the concepts you may also be doing crime or tort in the same examination)

If the case is one you may also want to use in an essay, be sure you understand any problems it raises or solves and / or the concept of law that is involved

Example

In **Brown**, the judges decided that consent was not a defence to serious harm, so this would apply to a scenario involving GBH and can be used in a criminal law problem question.

However, it can also be used in an essay question because it raises a problem in the law, as the reasoning was obscure. It was not sufficiently clear why the consent defence failed. It could be argued that the defence fails if harm was intended (this would apply to **s 18** but not **s 20**), or alternatively that the defence fails if harm was serious (this would apply to both **s 18** and **s 20**).

As regards the concept of balancing conflicting interests, the act occurred in private but in court the individuals' interests were subordinated to the public interest. It is debateable whether the public interest should have prevailed in such a case. It does not appear to satisfy either utilitarianism or distributive justice, as the burden on the men of a criminal conviction arguably outweighs any public benefit in the law being used to uphold some kind of morality.

Go through the essay pointers, examination tips and summaries of the topic. These provide a base of the essential points which may need to be addressed

Go to the examination board's website for past papers, mark schemes and reports

Practise answering questions then look at the examiners' mark schemes and reports to see if you were on the right track

Revision of balancing conflicting interests

Where interests are in conflict, the law will try to engineer a balance which will achieve social cohesion.

The purpose of the law is to satisfy as many interests as possible (the utilitarian view).

Society needs law to regulate the conflicts that arise between different interests. Law is a way of engineering how society behaves (Jhering).

Public and private interests should not be balanced against each other (Pound).

However, in practice neither Parliament nor the courts follow Pound's idea that you can only balance interests on the same level.

Any attempt to balance interests on different levels would mean the dominant interest prevails and this is likely to be the public one.

Some more examples of the public/private interest conflict

Human rights

One area of conflict between public and private interests is seen in the protection of human rights. Since the passing of the **Human Rights Act 1998**, incorporating the **European Convention on Human Rights** into English law, private interests have been given greater priority. However, a person's rights to, e.g., respect for a private and family life may restrict not only the freedom of another, but also the public interest because the person is a celebrity – as in the cases brought by Michael Douglas, Naomi Campbell and J. K. Rowling. Also, most of the Articles of the Convention have derogation clauses which specifically allow the public interest to take precedence in cases of national security, public safety and health. Thus even where the private interest is protected by legislation the public interest may still outweigh these interests. Overall it can be said that achieving a fair balance is not easy and there has been limited success in doing so.

Morals and conflicting interests

There is an overlap with morals and many cases such as **Quintavalle**, **Re A**, **Pretty** and **Purdy** can be discussed in an essay, as long as the emphasis changes to one involving the competing interests rather than the issue of morals. In cases like these the interests being balanced are not only those of the individual and the state but also those of other interest groups who feel strongly on the 'right to life' or 'right to choice' issues. Cases like this are useful in illustrating not only how the courts are required to balance competing interests, but also the difficulties in doing so. Where opinion on a subject is so divided it is almost impossible to satisfy the interests of any particular group and neither the courts nor Parliament are able successfully to resolve the conflict.

Procedure

Over the years, access to justice improved and other procedures were put in place to balance a person's interests against the state, or public interest. However more recently, there have been several changes to the criminal justice system which affect whether it is still possible to achieve an effective balance. For example, legal assistance has been reduced, the right to silence has been restricted and attempts have been made to restrict the right to jury trial, the public interest is proving dominant and individual rights are being eroded.

Task 7

In deciding how successful / effective the law is in balancing interests one can look at cases and situations where public interests and private interests conflict. Pound's view was that public and private interests should not be balanced against each other. Any attempt to balance interests on different levels would mean the dominant interest prevailed, which is likely to be the public interest.

Bearing this in mind, briefly state how effective you think the law is in balancing the conflicting interests in the following examples. After dealing with the examples add a brief conclusion on how successful the law has been overall in balancing interests.

Brown 1994

Mandatory life sentence for murder

The Consumer Protection Act 1987

Anti-terrorism laws

Watts v Herts CC

Conclusion

Examination tip

Many examination boards suggest you should use current issues and developments in the law when answering questions on jurisprudence or concepts of law. The examination question may even require recent examples, e.g., by asking why this concept is still important today. Keep an eye on current affairs and try to bring in some of your own ideas as to how far the law is, or should be, involved in balancing conflicting interests. Although there is no right answer to these issues if you offer your own opinion avoid being too opinionated. Remember this is a law examination, so always use the theories, cases, Acts of Parliament and / or legal procedures to support what you say.

Task 8

Find a copy of a recent newspaper and see if you can find any references to what could be described as a conflict of interest. Make a note of how the situation involves the law and how the interests have been or could be balanced. Keep a note of this as something you could refer to in an examination answer.

Examination practice

Although different examination boards have different ways of styling their examination papers, there are always going to be common elements. You will need to be able to apply the law you have learnt to a particular scenario and you will need to be able to evaluate a given topic to provide a critique of the law, including reforms where appropriate.

A general guide to examination papers

Read **all** questions carefully before deciding which to answer.

Look again at the ones you wish to answer to make sure you can do so and make brief notes. This can be a useful checklist later when you are tired and your memory begins to fail.

Structure your answer. A solid start is worth a lot and gets the examiner on your side. A small plan is helpful.

It is necessary to do more than regurgitate your notes. Never put in irrelevant material just because you know it – there is **never** a question asking you to 'write all you know about...'. You need to be selective as to what is relevant, and choose appropriate cases and examples in support of what you say.

In essay questions, you will usually be asked to form an opinion or to weigh up arguments for and against a particular statement. Here a broader range of knowledge is needed showing arguments for, arguments against and an evaluation of these arguments. You should always round off your answer with a short concluding paragraph, preferably using some of the wording from the question to indicate to the examiner that you are addressing the specific issue raised.

Essays should have a logical structure. The beginning should introduce the subject matter, the central part should explain / analyse / criticise it as appropriate, and the conclusion should bring the various strands of argument together with reference to the question set.

Try to consider alternative arguments. A well-rounded essay will bring in other views even if you disagree with them; you cannot shoot them down without setting them up first.

Here is an idea of how to structure your essay.

Writing a discussion essay: staging the information logically

If you stage your essay as follows, it will make it easy to read, logically structured and easier to write. It may also mean you don't leave out important points. Here's how it works:

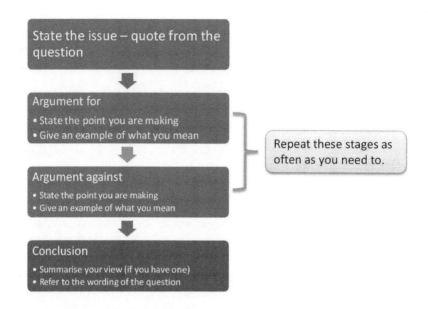

Writing each paragraph: making each one logical and easy to read (and write!)

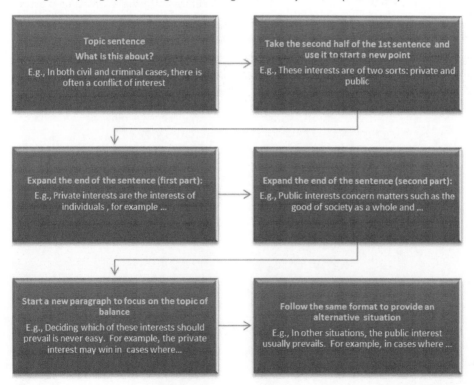

Finally, make sure you cover the whole question; there are only a certain number of marks available. The examiner has a mark scheme to work to, so however brilliant your answer to one part of the question is, missing out the other parts will severely reduce your total marks.

Examination practice for Balancing Conflicting Interests

Although different examination boards have different ways of styling their examination papers, there are always going to be common elements. You will need to be able to explain and evaluate a given concept to provide a critique of the area, including case examples and reference to theorists where appropriate.

Examination tip

There may be similarities in the questions on past papers, but look carefully at the wording to make sure you get the emphasis right. You can prepare a basic answer to a question but you will need to be able to adapt it to cover the specific point raised. It is important to make sure you answer the actual question, not the one you hoped to get which you saw in an earlier paper.

There are many areas of law and procedure that can be discussed in an essay on conflicting interests. It will also be necessary to examine the law in the chosen area so you can evaluate whether the law is effective in achieving a successful balance between the conflicting interests.

It is not always the case that the law even attempts to balance interests fairly. Rather than attempt a compromise between the conflicting interests, in some areas the law has been uncompromisingly supportive of one party especially where there is an issue of state security or in criminal cases involving child victims. Here the balance is tipped in favour of the state or the child.

The 'Essay pointers' and 'Examination tips' are intended to provide you with information to use in an essay. Look through these and your answers to the tasks before doing the examination practice below.

Essay pointer

One way to practise for an essay on this subject is to choose an issue that interests you and make a note of what the conflicting interests are and how they are balanced. Then consider how effective this balance is, with mention of a theory or two. If possible offer an opposing argument to show you have taken a balanced view of the issue.

Example

Taking assisted suicide as an example, there are conflicting interests between the person who wishes to die and people who are opposed to assisted suicide. Sometimes family members may not agree with the decision either. Pound might argue that only the interests of the person concerned and other individuals affected, such as family and friends, should be balanced against each other. It should be is a person's right to choose the time and manner of their own death. However both Parliament and the courts have taken into account the public interest when deciding that it should remain illegal to help someone to die. The courts may have done so more reluctantly but have indicated that on a matter such as this it is for an elected Parliament to change the law. This means the balance has not been effective for those who want help, as no-one has yet won a 'right to die' case. On a libertarian view of justice the law should allow assisted suicide as it does not harm others, only the individual concerned. On the other hand, an argument in favour of the public interest being taken into the balance is that society as a whole is harmed by any type of taking of life, so the law should not allow it. This would accord with the natural law view that law should have a moral content; therefore assisted suicide should remain illegal because the taking of life is s immoral.

Examination tip

Most questions on this area require a critical analysis of the different types of interest and an evaluation of whether, and how far, the law is effective striking an appropriate balance between conflicting interests. A strong answer would include a brief discussion of the theories and how these relate to the chosen area of law e.g., how Pound's view that interests should only be balanced on the same level can be supported by the imbalance that often occurs when the public is balanced against the private interest. On the other hand the utilitarian view that Pound built on looks at the greater good so this could favour the wider public interest.

Task 9 Examination practice

Give a very brief plan of how you should approach the answer to the following questions, taken from A-Level examination papers. They are very similar so you can just do one plan, but add a concluding paragraph for each to show how you would show you have addressed the specific question.

Discuss the extent to which the law is effective in balancing conflicting interests.

Consider how successful English law is in balancing conflicting interests.

To what extent can it be argued that law can be used effectively to enable an appropriate balance to be struck between conflicting interests?

Task 10 Examination practice

Write an essay (around 400 words) on whether you think judges and / or Parliament achieve an effective balance between conflicting interests. Include some reference to academic or judicial opinions or debates surrounding the particular area – and don't forget to use cases and examples in support of what you say.

Task 11 Examination question

Discuss the extent to which the law is effective in balancing conflicting interests.

This is included in the above task so you can use that plan and expand on it.

Answers to self-test questions and tasks

Task 1

This task only asked you to make some notes on new cases or procedure you have come across so the answer will depend on what you chose. Keep your notes to use as illustrations in an examination answer. Here is one possible example.

The **Protection of Freedoms Act 2012** reduced the time someone can be locked up without charge to 14 days. The interests which had to be balanced were those of an individual not to be locked up without charge against the public interest in being safe. These were balanced by deciding that someone can be locked up without charge (protecting the public interest) but reducing it to 14 days (protecting the private interest). Whether this is an appropriate balance and achieved justice is debateable either way. On the one hand it meets the needs of people in general to be kept safe by removing the threat of harm; on the other it seems harsh on the individual who may not have done anything wrong.

There are many other examples seen above which you could add so you will have a wide range.

Task 2

Aristotle's theory of distributive justice is that the law acts to distribute benefits and burdens fairly throughout society. This supports the decision in **Miller** because the award of an injunction would have meant that cricket could no longer be played and this would be a burden on society. The award of damages instead allowed a benefit to the claimant without imposing too great a burden on the local people and the club, thus providing a fair distribution.

Task 3

The answer will depend on your chosen case but here is an example.

In **Harris v Perry** a child was seriously injured on a bouncy castle at a children's party. The mother of the children giving the party was found to have breached her duty of care to provide adequate supervision, because she was not watching at the moment it happened. She appealed. The CA held that it would not be in the public interest to expect constant surveillance or supervision in a case like this, although where there was a high risk of serious harm there could be a duty to take greater care. The appeal was allowed. The court attempted to achieve a fair balance by looking at the risk of serious harm and deciding that this was not sufficient to expect constant supervision by the mother. As the CA also suggested that a duty could be breached where there was a high risk of harm this means justice can be achieved in a riskier situation by finding a reasonable person would have taken greater care. Overall the interests seem to have been balanced fairly as if children had to be supervised all the time parents might never allow a party.

Task 4

Again the answer will depend on which procedures you chose, here is one example.

In a criminal trial that deals with anything more than a summary offence the accused has a right to trial by jury. This balances the right of the individual (to a fair trial) against the public interest (the cost). A Utilitarian might say this achieves a fair balance as although it is more costly for society as a whole it is very important that a person has a mixed group of people deciding on what happened in the case and giving the final verdict, rather than a judge alone. The greater benefit is achieved by protecting the private interests of the accused. This can be supported by the fact that the law itself recognised the private interest should be dominant. An attempt to tip the balance in favour of the public interest by removing the right to a jury in complex fraud trials never became law and was formally repealed by the **Protection of Freedoms Act 2012**.

Task 5

There is no right answer to this but hopefully you made some notes. Here are a few possible discussion points. It is arguable that a Utilitarian would say that the interests of the many outweigh those of the few, so torture would be permissible. However this type of behaviour is against the rule of law and not acceptable in a fair and just society so it is also arguable that society as a whole is demeaned by allowing torture, a point made by Lord Hoffman in relation to the **Anti-terrorism, Crime and Security Act 2001**. Under this view the greater benefit to the greatest number of people is achieved by not allowing torture. Locking up people without charge or trial has been the focus of much debate and law. The interests of society to be protected have to be balanced not only against the suspect's rights, but also against justice as a whole. In this case there is a stronger argument than in the case of torture but it is still necessary to take into the balance the interests of those who have not been shown to have done wrong. The earlier anti-terrorism laws did not achieve a just balance but the **Protection from Freedom Act 2012** has reduced the time someone can be locked up without charge to 14 days. Perhaps this is now fair because even though it seems harsh on the person who may not have done anything wrong, society needs to be protected too.

Task 6

Aristotle's theory of distributive justice is that the law acts to distribute benefits and burdens fairly throughout society. This theory could be used to argue against the decision in **Miller** because Mrs Miller did not get much benefit, so the distribution was unfair. A small award of damages as compensation did not help her to be able to sit in her garden without being bombarded with cricket balls. A more effective balance could have been achieved by issuing an injunction to restrict the amount of cricket played. This would not be too great a burden on society as games could still be played at certain times, but at other times Mrs Miller could enjoy her garden in peace. This would distribute the burdens and benefits more fairly. Pound's theory could have produced a more appropriate outcome because he would have said that her private interests should not have been balanced against the public interest. If her private interest in enjoying her garden was merely balanced against the private interests of those playing cricket it is more likely a partial injunction would have been awarded to restrict the amount of games. This would balance the benefits and burdens more fairly.

Self-test questions

By saying that law is an engineering tool Pound means that the law can be used as a form of social control and to produce a balance between the different interests within society

There are plenty of examples and yours may well be different. Here's one from each area (you only needed one from the substantive law and one from the legal process)

*An example from tort is **Miller v Jackson** where the interests of the club and the local community in general were in conflict with Mrs Miller's interests.*

*An example from contract is the **Unfair Contract Terms Act** where the interests of the consumer (usually the weaker party to the contract) are in conflict with those of the business (the stronger party) who wants to impose terms and the law tries to correct the imbalance between them*

*An example from crime is **R v R** where the interests of the wife, and society in general, to be protected were in conflict with the interests of the husband not to be liable for something that was not a crime at the time*

An example from the legal process is the provision of bail which recognises D's right to freedom of movement so there is usually a presumption that bail should be allowed. However in murder cases the balance tips in favour of protecting society so the presumption is that bail will not be allowed.

The Human Rights Act has an effect on court cases because Judges must take human rights into account when interpreting laws

A Utilitarian would engineer the balance between conflicting interests by balancing the interests to ensure the greatest good for the greatest number of people

Mrs Miller was bothered by cricket balls dropping into her garden. The court balanced the interests between her and the club and society in general. She did not get the injunction she wanted to stop cricket being played but got financial compensation instead.

Task 7

Brown

The public interest, in protecting society from immoral or deviant behaviour, prevailed and the private interests of the defendants was subordinated to this. This can be compared to **Wilson** where the public did not need protection from such behaviour as it was seen as entirely private. It can, however, be argued that it is hard to reconcile these two cases so the law has been unsuccessful.

Mandatory life sentence for murder

The mandatory sentence is an attempt to protect the public interest in being safe from harm, but has been criticised by judges as preventing them from being fair to individual offenders. The public interest prevails at the expense of the individual and this supports Pound's view that public and private interests should not be balanced against each other.

The Consumer Protection Act 1987

The **Consumer Protection Act** helps to redress the imbalance between the individual consumer and businesses, which usually have more power. The Act establishes strict liability in respect of defective goods which cause harm to a consumer; in this case the law has been successful in balancing the competing interests and has developed the law as established in **Donoghue v Stevenson**.

Anti-terrorism laws

Laws dealing with the threat of terrorism have been controversial and some argue that here the law has not been effective in achieving a just balance as individual rights are suffering in the interests of state security, as people can be locked up without a trial, and may well be innocent. It can be argued that when state security is an issue the law cannot achieve an effective balance as the public interest will always prevail.

Watts v Herts CC

The dominant interest was the public interest, and the fireman's private interests were subordinated to this. This again supports Pound's view that public and private interests should not be balanced against each other. The attempt to balance interests on different levels meant the dominant public interest prevailed, and he received no compensation for his injuries.

Conclusion

In conclusion it can be seen that in most cases where public and private interests are in conflict it is the public interest that will prevail, which supports Pound's view that public and private interests should not be balanced against each other and suggests that the law has not been successful in achieving a fair balance.. On the other hand some attempt to effectively address an imbalance is seen in consumer protection laws and human rights law, so here the law has been more successful.

Task 8

The answer depends on what you found. Here is an example I found whilst writing this book. In September 2014 a nanny was employed for Prince George, who was born last year. Kensington palace has asked for her privacy to be protected and has said that illegal photographs taken in the palace grounds were a matter for the Royal Parks police. If the case goes to court the law will need to balance the public interest in the royal family against the nanny's private interest to a degree of privacy. For case examples on this balance see under the heading '**Privacy v freedom of expression**' and under '**Human Rights**' in the revision section.

Task 9

Your plan may be different as there are many ways to approach all the concepts of law questions. The following is a guide on which you can build. You would need to develop the points a little and expand on the examples as you did in the tasks.

As with most essays an explanation is needed as a basis for a later evaluation.

A brief plan would be:

> *An explanation of the different types of interests, with mention of theorists such as Pound*
>
> *Identification of appropriate areas of law, substantive and/or procedural, where interests might conflict*
>
> *Illustration, using examples, of the interests which may be in conflict*

Once a basic explanation (with examples) has been provided it then needs to be evaluated. This part of your plan should include:

> *An analysis and evaluation of the material explained above which focuses in particular on the ways in which the balance may be engineered (how did the court / Parliament decide on the matter?)*
>
> *An analysis of what might represent an 'appropriate' balance between the conflicting interests (how would Pound, Mill, Bentham etc. view the decision? You can add your own opinion as to what might be appropriate to this but relate it to one of the theories)*
>
> *An evaluation of the extent to which the law is effective in engineering a fair balance, again using examples (did the court / Parliament reach an appropriate decision / achieve justice?).*

Conclusions

Conclusion 1: In conclusion it can be seen that in most cases where public and private interests are in conflict it is the public interest that will prevail, which supports Pound's view that public and private interests should not be balanced against each other and suggests that the law has not been *effective in balancing conflicting interests to any great extent*. On the other hand some attempt to effectively address an imbalance is seen in consumer protection laws and human rights law, so here the law has been *effective in balancing conflicting interest to some extent*.

Conclusion 2: In conclusion it can be seen that in most cases where public and private interests are in conflict it is the public interest that will prevail, which supports Pound's view that public and private interests should not be balanced against each other and suggests that the law has not been *successful* in achieving a fair balance.. On the other hand some attempt to effectively address an imbalance is seen in consumer protection laws and human rights law, so here the law has been more *successful*.

Conclusion 3: In conclusion it can be seen that in most cases where public and private interests are in conflict it is the public interest that will prevail, which supports Pound's view that public and private interests should not be balanced against each other and suggests that *the law has not been used effectively to enable an appropriate balance to be struck between conflicting interests*. On the other hand some attempt to effectively address an imbalance is seen in consumer protection laws and human rights law, so here *the law has been used more effectively to engineer an appropriate balance.*

The three conclusions are very similar but in each case the examiner is reminded that the specific issue is being address by using the words from the question (given here in italics)

Task 10

Where there is a dispute between conflicting interests the law is needed to act as decision-maker. Pound suggested that only interests on the same level should be balanced and one can see from several cases where this has not occurred that the law does not always get the balance right. An example is **Latimer v AEC** where the public interest in keeping the factory open prevailed but this meant the claimant received no compensation. In **Miller v Jackson** the claimant again received no effective remedy because the public interest prevailed. All nuisance cases involve "*striking a balance between the interests of neighbours*" (**Hunter v Canary Wharf**), and sometimes the law is more effective. In **Christie v Davey,** the law was quite effective in balancing the conflicting interests of the two neighbours. They were both interfering with the others' enjoyment, but on balance the law favoured the person who did not act out of malice. There were several conflicting interests in **Quintavalle** where the court had to make a ruling on the issue of whether a couple could select an embryo with certain characteristics, what is often termed 'designer babies'. The court was perhaps a little more effective in balancing the interests here as it ruled that tissue typing could be done but should be decided by the embryology organisation on a case-by-case basis. This was attempting to satisfy the most interests so would be supported by Utilitarians. However natural law would be against it as it would be seen as immoral. It is not only the courts but Parliament that attempts to balance conflicting interests. An example is the **Consumer Protection Act** which was put in place in order to protect consumers who have suffered harm due to a faulty product. A consumer is usually in a weaker position with fewer resources than a manufacturer. The Act addressed this imbalance between the parties by tipping the balance in favour of the consumer, who no longer has to prove fault.

Overall it can be said that the law sometimes gets the balance right, but is less effective in balancing conflicting interests when the public interest is balanced against the private. Also, when an attempt is made to satisfy too many interests, as happens in emotive case like **Quintavalle** and **Re A**, it is possible none will actually be satisfied. Deciding on a case-by-case basis means the law will be less certain, and if it is inconsistent the law cannot be said to be effective.

Task 11 Examination question

Here is the plan from Task 9 again

An explanation of the different types of interests, with mention of theorists such as Pound

Identification of appropriate areas of law, substantive and/or procedural, where interests might conflict

Illustration, using examples, **of the interests which may be in conflict**

An analysis and evaluation of the material explained above which focuses in particular on the ways in which the balance may be engineered

An analysis of what might represent an 'appropriate' balance between the conflicting interests.

An evaluation of the extent to which the law is effective in engineering a fair balance again using examples

An explanation of the different types of interests, with mention of theorists such as Pound

Reference to private and public interests

Pound's theory of law as an engineering tool to balance interests and guide the way society behaves

Reference to utilitarianism or other theories of justice as they relate to balancing conflicting interests

See tasks 2, 3 and 4

Identification of appropriate areas of law, substantive and/or procedural, where interests might conflict

Explain how interests might conflict in crime, contract, tort and legal process. Possibly add remedies and defences

Illustration, using examples, of the interests which may be in conflict

This carries on from the above but expands on a few of the examples in more detail

Include something from current affairs and/or human rights to get your essay up-to-date.

See under 'current affairs' and revision plus tasks 5 and 8

An analysis and evaluation of the material explained above which focuses in particular on the ways in which the balance may be engineered

Analyse how the conflicting interests were balanced by Parliament or the courts in your examples

Discuss *how* the law engineered the balance in the examples used above (e.g., did the public interest prevail, were the interests balanced fairly?), and how it can be used to engineer how society behaves (e.g., to stop people smoking, not to produce faulty goods, not to harm others)

To evaluate you need to produce a balanced argument – see tasks 2 and 6

An analysis of what might represent an 'appropriate' balance between the conflicting interests

See tasks 1, 2, 3 and 6

An evaluation of the extent to which the law is effective in engineering a fair balance, again using examples

Reference to tasks 1, 2, 3 and 6 and whether the appropriate balance was actually achieved

See tasks 7 and 10

Conclusion

See task 10

Appendix: Abbreviations and acknowledgements

The following abbreviations are commonly used. You may use them in an examination answer, but write them in full the first time, e.g., write 'actual bodily harm (ABH)' and then after that you can just write 'ABH'.

General

Draft Code – A Criminal Code for England and Wales (Law Commission No. 177), 1989

CCRC Criminal Cases Review Commission

ABH actual bodily harm

GBH grievous bodily harm

D defendant

C claimant

V Victim

CA Court of Appeal

HL House of Lords

SC Supreme Court

Acts

S – section (thus **s 1** Theft Act 1968 refers to section 1 of that Act)

s 1(2) means section 1 subsection 2 of an Act.

OAPA – Offences against the Person Act 1861

In cases – these don't need to be written in full

CC (at beginning) chief constable

CC (at end) county council

BC borough council

DC district council

LBC London borough council

AHA Area Health Authority

J Justice

LJ Lord Justice

LCJ Lord Chief Justice

LC Lord Chancellor

AG Attorney General

CPS Crown Prosecution Service

DPP Director of Public Prosecutions

AG Attorney General